EARTH'S
NATURAL
BIOMES

TUNDRA
BIOMES

Louise and Richard Spilsbury

Crabtree Publishing Company
www.crabtreebooks.com

Crabtree Publishing Company
www.crabtreebooks.com
1-800-387-7650

Published in Canada
Crabtree Publishing
616 Welland Avenue
St. Catharines, ON
L2M 5V6

Published in the United States
Crabtree Publishing
PMB 59051
350 Fifth Ave, 59th Floor
New York, NY 10118

Published in 2018 by CRABTREE PUBLISHING COMPANY.

First published in 2017 by Wayland
Copyright © Wayland, 2017

Authors: Louise Spilsbury, Richard Spilsbury

Editors: Hayley Fairhead, Philip Gebhardt

Design: Smart Design Studio

Map (page 7) by Stefan Chabluk

Editorial director: Kathy Middleton

Proofreader: Lorna Notsch

Prepress technician: Tammy McGarr

Print and production coordinator: Margaret Amy Salter

Photographs

All photographs except where mentioned supplied by
Nature Picture Library www.naturepl.com

p4 and title page(main) Andy Trowbridge; p5(main), cover(main) and title page(tr) Klein & Hubert; p5(inset) Phil Savoie; p6 Phillippe Clement; p7 Neil Lucas; p8, front cover(b) and title page(b) Alex Hyde; p9 and p32(t) Paul Harcourt Davies; p10 and p30(t) Erlend Haarberg; p11(main) Asgeir Helgestad; p12 and imprint page(b) Doug Wechsler; p13 and p32(b) Sergey Gorshkov; p14 and p30(b) Erland Haarberg; p15 Ingo Arndt; p16 Sergey Gorshkov; p17 Jenny E. Ross; p18 Eric Baccega; p19 Markus Varesvuo; p20(main), front cover(tl) and contents(t) Wild Wonders of Europe / Lesniewski; p20(inset) Robert Thompson; p21 David Welling; p22 and contents(b) Eric Baccega; p23 and p31(t) Eric Baccega; p24, front cover(main) and p31(b) Steven Kazlowski; p25, p26, p27 and p28 Bryan and Cherry Alexander; p29, back cover(tl) and imprint page(t) Ingo Arndt.

Photographs supplied by Shutterstock: back cover(tr) and p11(inset) Bildagentur Zoonar GmbH; p27(inset) Karl Umbriaco.

Every attempt has been made to clear copyright. Should there be any inadvertent omission, please apply to the publisher for rectification.

The website addresses (URLs) included in this book were valid at the time of going to press. However, it is possible that contents or addresses may have changed since the publication of this book. No responsibility for any such changes can be accepted by either the author or the Publisher.

Printed in the USA/122019/BG20171102

Library and Archives Canada Cataloguing in Publication

Spilsbury, Louise, author
    Tundra biomes / Louise Spilsbury, Richard Spilsbury.

(Earth's natural biomes)
Includes index.
Issued in print and electronic formats.
ISBN 978-0-7787-3997-5 (hardcover).--
ISBN 978-0-7787-4182-4 (softcover).--
ISBN 978-1-4271-2007-6 (HTML)

    1. Tundra ecology--Juvenile literature. 2. Tundras--Juvenile literature. I. Spilsbury, Richard, 1963-, author II. Title.

QH541.5.T8S67 2018   j577.5'86   C2017-906897-0
                                               C2017-906898-9

Library of Congress Cataloging-in Publication Data

Names: Spilsbury, Louise, author. | Spilsbury, Richard, 1963- author.
Title: Tundra biomes / Louise Spilsbury, Richard Spilsbury.
Description: New York, New York : Crabtree Publishing, [2018] |
    Series: Earth's natural biomes | Includes index. |
Identifiers: LCCN 2017051159 (print) | LCCN 2017056359 (ebook) |
    ISBN 9781427120076 (Electronic HTML) |
    ISBN 9780778739975 (reinforced library binding) |
    ISBN 9780778741824 (pbk.)
Subjects: LCSH: Tundra ecology--Juvenile literature. |
    Tundras--Conservation--Juvenile literature.
Classification: LCC QH541.5.T8 (ebook) | LCC QH541.5.T8 S65 2018
    (print) | DDC 577.5/86--dc23
LC record available at https://lccn.loc.gov/2017051159

CONTENTS

WHAT IS TUNDRA?

Tundra is a cold, dry, and barren **biome**. The word *tundra* comes from a word meaning treeless plain in the Finnish language, and the most obvious thing about tundra is that there are no trees.

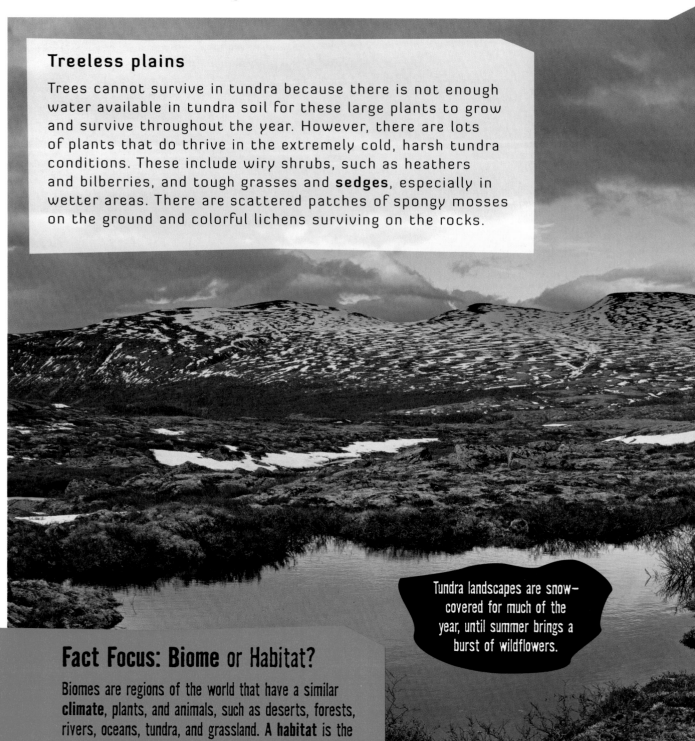

Treeless plains

Trees cannot survive in tundra because there is not enough water available in tundra soil for these large plants to grow and survive throughout the year. However, there are lots of plants that do thrive in the extremely cold, harsh tundra conditions. These include wiry shrubs, such as heathers and bilberries, and tough grasses and **sedges**, especially in wetter areas. There are scattered patches of spongy mosses on the ground and colorful lichens surviving on the rocks.

Tundra landscapes are snow-covered for much of the year, until summer brings a burst of wildflowers.

Fact Focus: Biome or Habitat?

Biomes are regions of the world that have a similar **climate**, plants, and animals, such as deserts, forests, rivers, oceans, tundra, and grassland. **A habitat** is the specific place in a biome where a plant or animal lives.

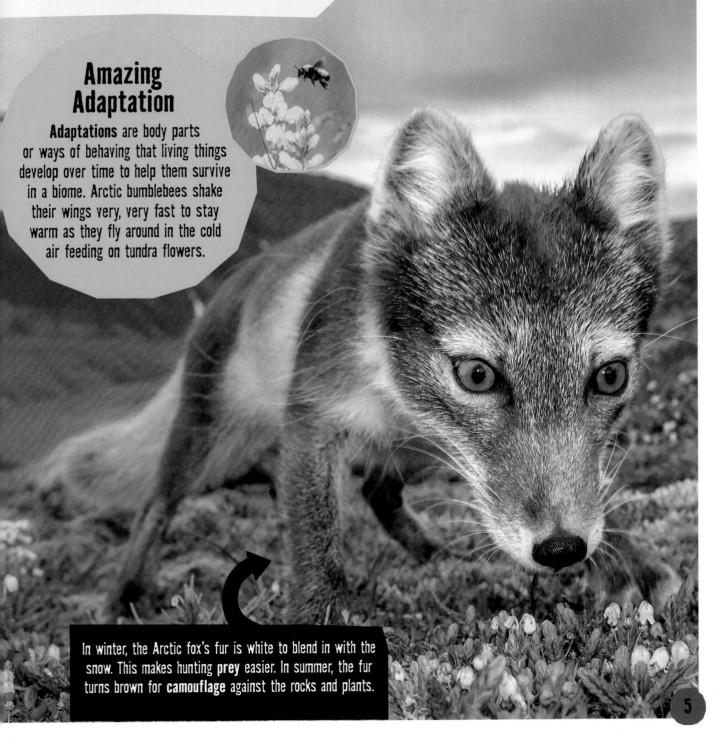

Tundra survivors

Many animals manage to survive in the challenging tundra biome. The low plants are teeming with animal life, from spiders and midges to moths and bumblebees. Some of these help to **pollinate** the flowers, so they can produce seeds and berries. Hares, lemmings, geese, mountain goats, and **caribou** feast on the tundra plants.

Hunters in the tundra

Tundra is a hunting ground for lots of **predators**. In the air, eagles and owls fly silently, on the lookout for a tasty bird or mammal to catch and eat. On the ground, tundra predators can be as small as shrews or foxes, or as large as wolves and bears.

Amazing Adaptation

Adaptations are body parts or ways of behaving that living things develop over time to help them survive in a biome. Arctic bumblebees shake their wings very, very fast to stay warm as they fly around in the cold air feeding on tundra flowers.

In winter, the Arctic fox's fur is white to blend in with the snow. This makes hunting **prey** easier. In summer, the fur turns brown for **camouflage** against the rocks and plants.

WHERE IS TUNDRA FOUND?

The tundra biome covers over one-tenth of our planet's surface. Most tundra is in **Arctic** regions, but some is at the top of mountains.

Arctic lands

The Arctic is a region of Earth centered on the North Pole. Arctic tundra is the land surrounding the Arctic Ocean and covers the northernmost parts of northern Canada, Alaska, Greenland, Iceland, Sweden, Norway, Finland, and Russia. There is only 10 inches (25 cm) of actual rainfall each year, which falls during the milder summers.

The rest of the year it snows, and the snow freezes on the land. Most water in the soil is frozen for much of the year. Tree roots cannot draw up enough water to survive or grow deep enough roots to support the tall structure of a tree.

Fact Focus: Treelines

Bordering the tundra, there is often a **treeline**. This marks the slightly warmer and wetter conditions where trees can survive. Adjacent to the Arctic tundra, much of the forest is coniferous forest. This northern forest biome is called the boreal forest.

At this treeline in Alaska, there is no straight line of conifers marking the end of the boreal forest and the start of the tundra. Instead, trees are dotted among the pink bilberry and heather plants.

Arctic seasons

If you visited Arctic tundra you would need to wrap up warm all year round. Winter temperatures can drop to a freezing -25°F (-32°C), but even in summer it is very chilly. Winters are dark, cold, and windy, and last for over half the year. Summers are short, but also very light. The northern part of Earth tilts toward the Sun in summer, so the Arctic is sunlit for 24 hours a day. No wonder it is called the Land of the Midnight Sun!

Alpine tundra

A smaller part of the global tundra is found below the tops of high mountains. Temperatures decrease the higher up a mountain you go. At high altitudes, it is too windy and cold for many plants to survive. Alpine tundra can be found in mountains in cold regions, such as the Himalayas or Alps, but also at the tops of the tallest mountains in hot regions, such as Africa. Alpine tundra starts higher up mountains in warmer parts of the world.

On Mount Kenya, alpine tundra plants, such as giant groundsel, survive cold nights by closing their leaves to trap moisture and stop freezing or drying out.

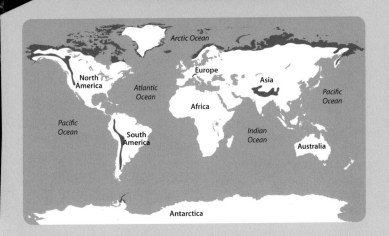

The purple areas on this map show where the tundra biome is found around the world.

7

ALPINE TUNDRA

Can you imagine living at the top of a cold, windy mountain?
Plants need very special adaptations, or features,
to help them survive there.

Surviving in the soil

There is little soil on mountain tops and steep, open slopes because the soil is blasted away by strong winds. Most plants live on gentle slopes where some soil has built up. Others survive in the thin pockets of soil trapped among the exposed rocks of mountain tops. Plants here rely on snow cover for **insulation** against the cold and to provide water when the snow melts.

Holding tight

Many alpine tundra plants survive the harsh winds by huddling together and making themselves smaller. Mosses grow in compact clumps close to the ground and out of the wind. This tight huddle traps moisture and warmth to help the plants protect each other and grow successfully.

Moss campion plants are cushion-shaped with overlapping leaves to trap warmth. Their flowers are raised above the plant, so insects can pollinate them easily.

Hairy plants

In the cold, the hairs on our arms stand up to trap warm air.
Some alpine tundra plants use the same technique to survive.
Edelweiss plants have a thick, woolly layer of fine strands
rather like hairs all over their leaves. The hairy leaves trap heat
and protect the plant from the strong sunlight.

Amazing Adaptation

In spring, the dark surface of the flower **buds** absorbs the heat of the sunlight that reaches them through a thin layer of snow. This speeds up the melting of the snow.

The dark color of alpine snowbell buds helps the flowers emerge from the snow early, so they have time to attract insects and produce seeds before winter returns.

Fact File: Northeast Greenland Biosphere Reserve

Location: Greenland
Size: 375,000 square miles (972,000 km²)
Overview: The largest **national park** in the world, where tundra animals, such as muskox, polar bears, walrus, snowy owls, and ptarmigans, far outnumber people.

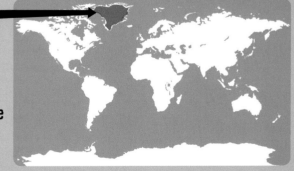

ARCTIC TUNDRA

Arctic tundra has one enormous difference from alpine tundra that is hidden beneath the surface—frozen soil, or **permafrost**.

A view of Arctic tundra from the air in summer shows how the land, with its gray rocks and brown grasses, has many pools and patterns made by soil that has been frozen and thawed many times.

Permafrost

Dig down 6 inches (15 cm) or so into Arctic tundra soil and your spade will start to hit hard permafrost, which is thousands of feet (hundreds of meters) deep over most of the Arctic. The permafrost stays frozen all year round, but during the Arctic summers, a depth of up to 10 feet (3 m) thaws. The **meltwater** then makes tundra soil extremely **boggy**.

Summer growth

Arctic tundra plants make the most of the warmth of summer. Many types of plants flower within days of the snow melting in spring and produce seeds in just over a month. Others, such as heathers, do not produce seeds every year, but spread by growing underground stems through the **thawing** soil.

Growing low

Tundra plants are mostly short to stop them being knocked over by winds. For example, the Arctic willow is related to tall willow trees of warmer biomes, but it is usually less than 12 inches (30 cm) tall and grows horizontally, covering many yards (meters) of ground.

Lichens are formed by a partnership between spongy **fungi** and tiny plant-like **algae**. The fungi support and protect the algae; the algae make food for the fungi. In Arctic tundra, some lichens, such as reindeer lichens, form a crust over many rocks and soil. They can grow all year round in low temperatures and survive being completely frozen and dried out for years.

Caribou can sniff out lichens buried up to 2 feet (60 cm) under snow. They dig it up using their hooves and antlers.

Amazing Adaptation

Caribou are one of the few animals that can survive on **lichens**. **Bacteria** in their stomachs help them break down this unusual food and get energy from it.

SURVIVING THE COLD

Tundra animals have some surprising and ingenious ways of surviving in a place where temperatures are as cold as most freezers.

Smaller is better

Many tundra animals have smaller body parts than usual. For example, animals in the Arctic, such as hares, foxes, wolves, and bears, have small ears, legs, and even tails in comparison to similar animals in warmer places. The reason is that body parts with a smaller **surface area** lose heat more slowly than parts with a larger surface area.

Wood frogs can survive being frozen in winter. They stop breathing and their hearts stop beating for weeks at a time, until the ice melts and they emerge again in spring!

Stop freezing

Most living things are nearly three-quarters water, and in freezing tundra conditions this water could turn to ice, which can cause damage to body **tissues**. Some tundra animals, including mosquitoes and frogs, make their own **antifreeze** chemicals. These stop the water in their bodies from freezing, so they can survive the bitter cold.

Amazing Adaptation

Wood frogs lay their eggs in water. If tundra ponds freeze before their eggs hatch, the jelly of the frogspawn freezes fast. This sucks water out of the developing frog inside so it survives the chill.

Warm coats

If you visited a tundra biome in winter, you would dress warmly. Many tundra mammals, including wolves, foxes, and lemmings, have a permanent warm coat of hair. Musk ox are giants of the tundra that keep warm even when covered with snow, thanks to their shaggy coat of long hair. Each hair is hollow and fatter at the tip than at the base. This special shape traps a layer of air warmed by the animal's body. The trapped air insulates an ox's skin from the cold air outside.

The outer hairs are very long and waterproof, too. This forms a kind of warming tent around the ox's body.

The musk ox's large, hard hooves also help it survive. During the winter months, the musk ox uses its hooves to break through ice, so it can drink the water underneath.

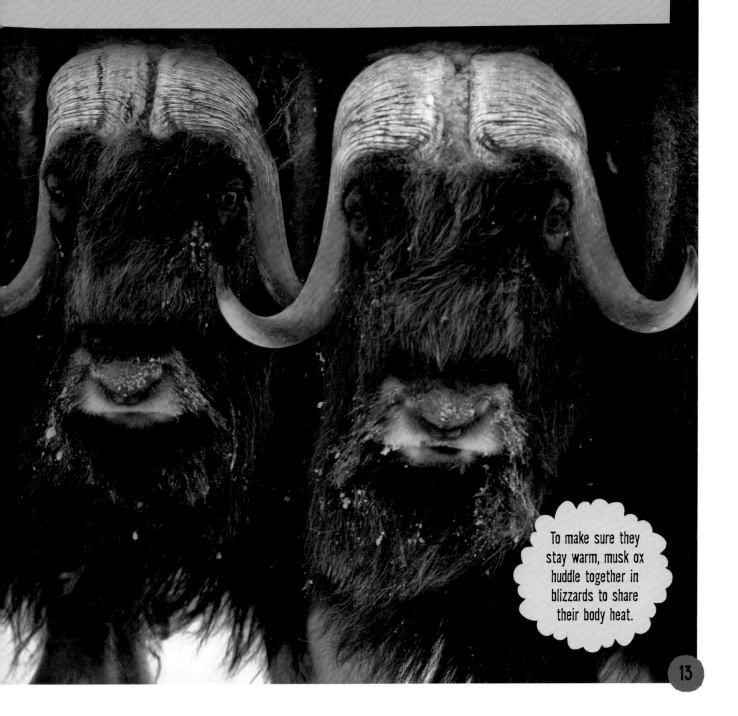

To make sure they stay warm, musk ox huddle together in blizzards to share their body heat.

GOING UNDERGROUND

Some tundra animals escape the harsh winters by staying in the same area, but going underground to stay warm.

A sticky situation

Lemmings are animals the size of a small guinea pig. They usually keep out of sight of predators by running about the tundra in tunnels and resting in burrows. In summer, the burrows are under deep grass or shrubs, but in winter they are under the snow.

Groups of lemmings choose deep but loose snow to burrow into, rather than snow that is packed firmly. The loose snow traps air, making it a better insulation layer. Temperatures in burrows under the soft snow blanket are about 12 degrees Fahrenheit (7 degrees Celsius) warmer than the temperature of the air above the snow.

If a predator comes near a lemming outside the burrow, the plucky little animal shrieks and runs at it with teeth bared to try to scare it off!

Fact Focus: Finding a New Home

In summer, hundreds of lemmings sometimes leave their underground hiding places and move to new places on the surface. This happens if so many young have been born that there is not enough food to go around in their current home.

Shutting down

Other tundra animals spend winter in a sleep-like state called **hibernation**. They prepare for this by stuffing themselves with enough food to get fat and by making a burrow where they will remain warm and hidden.

Arctic ground squirrels fatten up on roots, seeds, berries, and grasses. They line their burrows with dry grasses, fur, moss, and sedges. Then they settle down for winter and go into a deep sleep. During hibernation their hearts slow down from 400 beats per minute to 10, their body cools, and they breathe more slowly. They use 98 percent less energy by hibernating than by staying awake through winter.

Amazing Adaptation

Brown bears do not hibernate, but they do spend the winter months in a den. They go in and out of a deep sleep and survive mostly by using up their body fat. By spring, many have lost a third of their body weight.

Arctic ground squirrels like this one spend up to seven months of the tundra year curled up in hibernation in their burrows.

SEASONAL CHANGES

When spring and summer arrive in the Arctic tundra, there is a transformation from snowy wasteland to busy biome.

Moving in

With warmer weather, the snow melts. Plants grow new shoots, and masses of insects, such as flies, emerge from winter resting places, **breed**, and lay eggs. Some animals, such as caribou and geese, **migrate** to the tundra in spring from places with warmer winters to feed on the young plants. They may return to the same feeding grounds each year.

Raising young

Birds, such as terns and plovers, migrate to quiet tundra areas in spring and summer to have their young. They make nests from grasses on the snow-free land. The chicks that hatch feed on insects and new shoots. Within a few months, the young birds are ready to fly and migrate to warmer places farther south to escape the chills of winter.

Snow geese make nests on the thawed tundra land to rear their young. They need to keep careful watch to stop Arctic foxes from stealing their precious eggs.

Changing coats

Some tundra animals that do not migrate mark the seasons with a change in look. The fur coats of Arctic hares and foxes turn white for winter. This camouflage lets them match the color of the snowy landscape and remain hidden from other animals. For the hare, this is to stop them being eaten by foxes. For the fox, their camouflage helps them to approach prey, such as Arctic hares, without being noticed!

In spring when the snow melts, these animals' coats change to brown or gray so that they can be camouflaged by the rocks and plants. The darker coat helps them hunt or avoid being hunted during the days and light nights of summer.

Amazing Adaptation

Arctic hares have long, strong claws on their front paws. They use these to scratch away hard snow and free the twigs of the Arctic willow they like to eat. A hare's big back feet act like snowshoes to stop the animal from sinking into the snow.

Arctic hares use camouflage to hide from predators, such as snowy owls.

TUNDRA LIFE CYCLES

Getting the timing right in having young can make the difference between survival and death in the tundra.

Protecting babies

Some tundra animals go to great lengths to protect their vulnerable babies from the cold winters. A pregnant polar bear spends summer feeding and fattening up by eating seals. In autumn, she walks inland and digs out a den big enough for her to turn around in within a snowdrift or bank of soft soil. She waits for snow to shut her inside the den.

The polar bear usually gives birth to two cubs in November or December. She feeds the cubs with her milk for around three months before they are strong enough to leave the den in warmer spring weather. Then the cubs and mother head off for the long walk to find food.

Toward the end of the cubs' time in the den, the mother may go on brief, local hunting trips for snacks, such as Arctic hares or lemmings, to share with her babies.

Fact File: Wapusk National Park

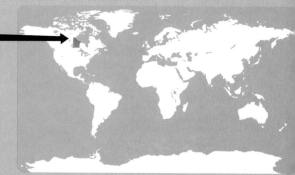

Location: Manitoba, Canada
Size: 4,430 square miles (11,475 km²)
Overview: One of the best places on Earth to see polar bears emerging from dens in the spring, but also thousands of caribou and rare birds, such as great gray owls and sandhill cranes.

More or less

Some tundra animals only ever have young if there is enough food to feed them. Snowy owls lay fewer eggs in summers when they cannot find enough lemmings to eat. Lemmings are the favorite prey of snowy owls (even though they also eat other animals, such as ducklings). In an average year, a snowy owl may eat 1,600 lemmings!

In years when there are few lemmings, the owls will not make nests or lay any eggs at all. Instead, they fly off to live in the nearest forest where there is a wider range of prey.

Snowy owl chicks are big, fluffy, and very hungry. They cannot survive unless the parents can find enough food to feed them.

Fact Focus: Snowy Owl Parents

Snowy owls usually mate for life. They share duties—hunting day and night to feed their young—and will defend their babies against any predators, even wolves.

EAT OR BE EATEN

The animals of any biome rely on each other for survival.
Food chains tell the story of who eats whom in a tundra biome.

Start of the chain

Plants start all food chains. Tundra plants trap the energy in sunlight in their leaves using the process of **photosynthesis**. This makes sugary food for the plant using carbon dioxide from the air and water. Plants use this food to fuel their growth. This slows or stops during long winters, when there is much less sunlight.

Amazing Adaptation

Hairs on alpine butterwort leaves have sticky tips that trap tiny tundra flies. The leaves release chemicals that **dissolve** the trapped insects and then soak up this fly soup as extra food.

Plant eaters

The tundra animals that eat plants range from tiny insects called springtails to massive musk ox. Eating and digesting leaves, stems, berries, and other parts of plants releases energy and **nutrients**. So, the energy transfers from plant to plant eater to help the animals stay healthy, grow, develop, and produce young.

The alpine ibex is totally reliant on eating alpine plants for its survival.

Meat eaters

When other tundra animals eat the plant eaters, energy transfers from the plant eaters to the meat eaters. Tundra spiders spin webs on plants to catch flies, and Arctic wolves work in teams to kill large musk oxen. When prey are not easy to find, tundra hunters may scavenge by eating any dead animals or remains they find. Maggots, worms, and slugs eat the leftovers of hunters and **scavengers**.

End of the chain

All food chains end with **decomposers**. These are bacteria and fungi that break down dead animal remains, dung, dead leaves, and other natural waste into nutrients. Nutrients in the tundra soil help plants grow and remain healthy. Energy transfers back to the soil to keep the food chain going.

A wolf defends the deer it has caught from hungry tundra scavengers.

Fact Focus: Food Webs

Every biome has hundreds of food chains that are connected in **food webs**. For example, grass is eaten by Arctic hares, lemmings, and brown bears. Brown bears eat Arctic hares and lemmings. Arctic wolves and snowy owls eat Arctic hares. Arctic wolves eat snowy owls.

PEOPLE IN THE TUNDRA

The tundra may be one of the coldest, toughest biomes on Earth, but there are many groups of people living in tundra habitats.

Tundra living

Groups of **Indigenous** people, such as Nenets and Inuit, have lived in the Arctic tundra for thousands of years. They have traditionally survived by hunting for food, such as seal meat, and wearing sealskin clothing. Some Nenets people of Siberia migrate with herds of caribou between winter and summer feeding grounds. These Nenets keep the caribou healthy and safe from wolves. They also kill caribou to eat the meat and drink the blood.

Changing societies

In the Arctic tundra, many Indigenous people's ways of life have changed. They often use **snowmobiles** to get around rather than dogsleds. Many people live in busy towns and cities, such as Cape Dorset in Canada, and they may work in shops, restaurants, and industries instead of hunting and selling caribou.

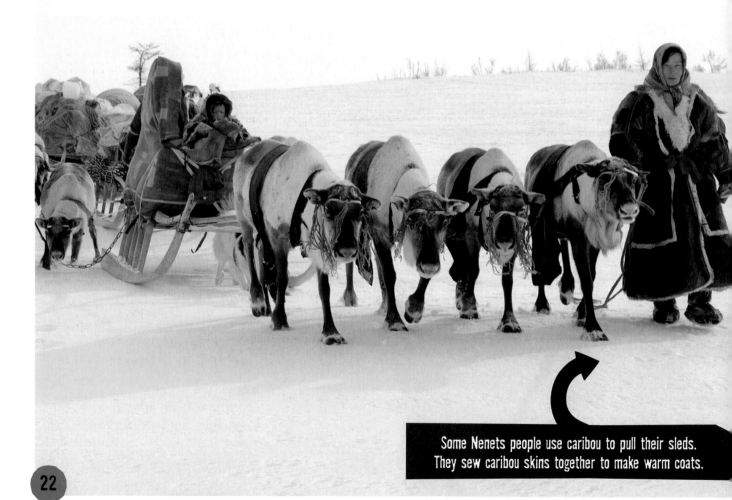

Some Nenets people use caribou to pull their sleds. They sew caribou skins together to make warm coats.

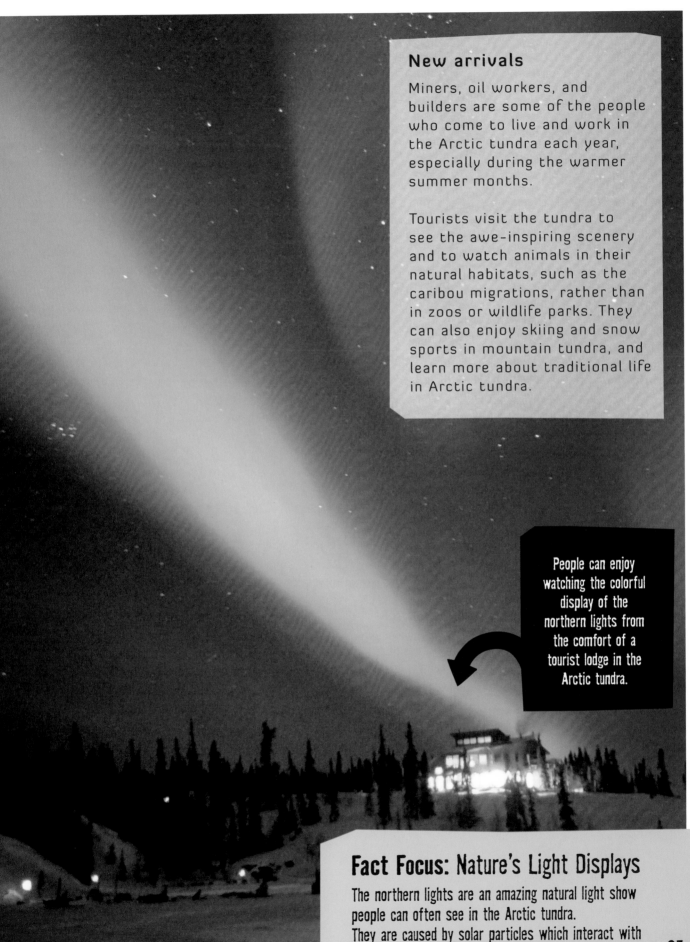

New arrivals

Miners, oil workers, and builders are some of the people who come to live and work in the Arctic tundra each year, especially during the warmer summer months.

Tourists visit the tundra to see the awe-inspiring scenery and to watch animals in their natural habitats, such as the caribou migrations, rather than in zoos or wildlife parks. They can also enjoy skiing and snow sports in mountain tundra, and learn more about traditional life in Arctic tundra.

People can enjoy watching the colorful display of the northern lights from the comfort of a tourist lodge in the Arctic tundra.

Fact Focus: Nature's Light Displays

The northern lights are an amazing natural light show people can often see in the Arctic tundra.
They are caused by solar particles which interact with Earth's magnetic field.

TUNDRA RESOURCES

In the tundra, people can collect wild foods, such as fish and berries, but there are also valuable **natural resources** deep beneath its surface.

Energy resources

Around one-fifth of the world's oil and gas are hidden under the Arctic region. These **fossil fuels** formed from ancient sea creatures that were squashed and heated inside deep, heavy layers of rock for millions of years.

Oil is made into fuel, which is burned in engines to power cars, trains, ships, and airplanes. Gas is burned in power stations to make electricity and also to heat homes. Companies dig deep wells in the Arctic tundra to get oil and gas from underground. They move the fossil fuels through very long pipelines or by ships to places where more people live.

The Trans-Alaskan oil pipeline snakes for thousands of miles (kilometers) across the Arctic tundra biome.

Fact Focus: Caribou Crossing

Oil and gas pipelines are raised on **stilts** where they cross caribou migration routes. The caribou can then continue on their way without having to climb over giant pipes.

24

Minerals

Fossil fuels are not the only hidden resources in the tundra. People also mine rich deposits of minerals, such as diamonds and amethyst, and metals from rocks at the surface and beneath the permafrost. The metals include iron, which is vital for making steel, and titanium, which is used to make aircraft bodies, computers, and golf clubs!

History in ice

Tundra permafrost is an important resource for scientists. They drill into permafrost to collect samples of ancient soil. Studying the soil can help scientists know what the tundra biome was like in the past. Bubbles of air trapped in ice reveal secrets about Earth's atmosphere thousands of years ago. Sometimes people even find frozen fossils of ancient animals, such as mammoths, when permafrost melts.

People use giant, heavy machines to mine rock rich in iron minerals in the tundra.

TUNDRA THREATS

The tundra is important and also very useful to people, but we are at risk of damaging it and destroying parts of it forever.

Melting permafrost

Temperatures on Earth are rising because of **global warming**. This is changing climates worldwide and causing more Arctic ice to melt each year. As permafrost melts, the soil is getting softer, deeper down. This is causing buildings and roads to sink into the ground. The melting is also releasing gases that were trapped in bubbles in frozen soil and gases that bacteria make when eating thawed-out plant waste. These gases are causing more global warming.

Melting permafrost affects animals too. For example, caribou have broad, soft hooves to walk on snow without sinking. But global warming is melting snow in the tundra earlier in the year, so migrating caribou end up walking on hard, painful rock instead.

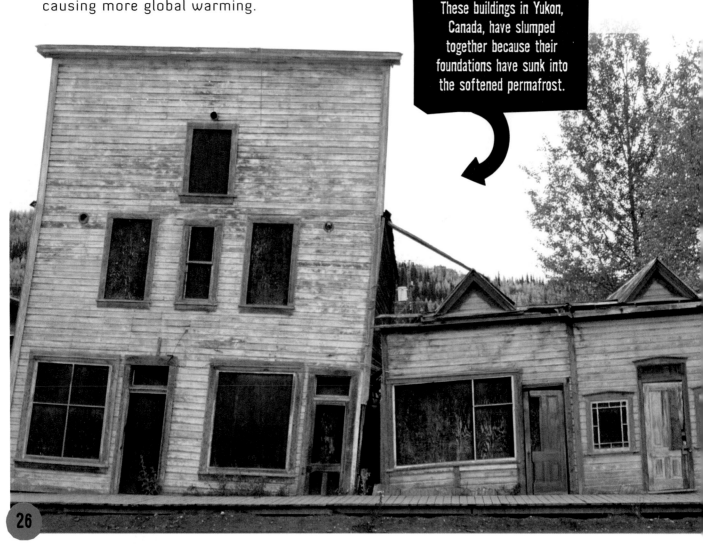

These buildings in Yukon, Canada, have slumped together because their foundations have sunk into the softened permafrost.

Pollution problems

Pollution is also a problem in the tundra. When oil spills from pipelines or chemicals used to process metals wash from mines, living things are harmed or even die. People spray chemicals called **pesticides** to kill irritating mosquitoes near tundra towns in summer. Unfortunately, the pesticides also poison tundra birds when they eat lots of mosquitoes.

Damage done

When the tundra landscape is damaged, it is slow to recover. Major damage is caused by building new roads, railways, mines, and towns. But even minor damage, such as bike or snow mobile tracks, ski runs, and footprints can take centuries to recover. This is because the top layer of soil washes away as the permafrost melts below.

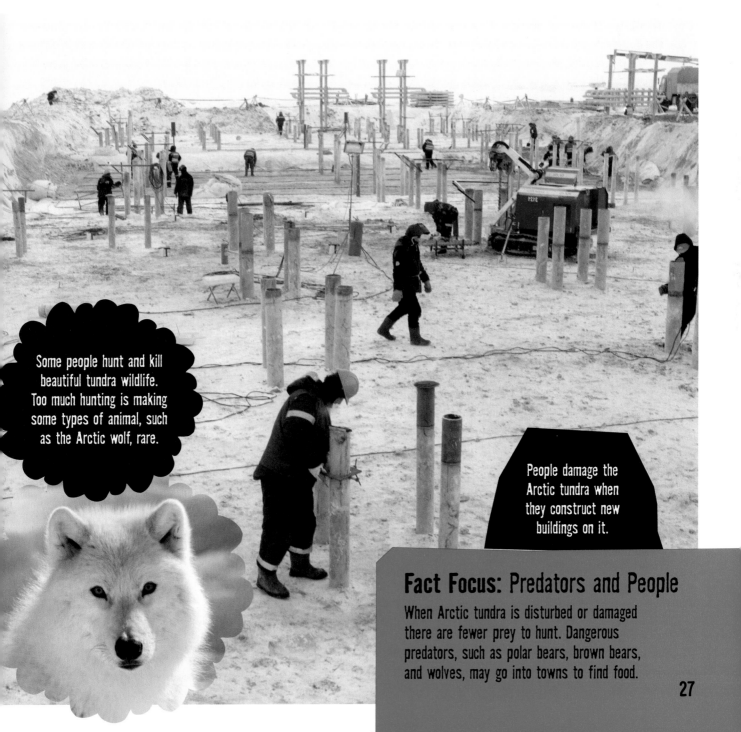

Some people hunt and kill beautiful tundra wildlife. Too much hunting is making some types of animal, such as the Arctic wolf, rare.

People damage the Arctic tundra when they construct new buildings on it.

Fact Focus: Predators and People

When Arctic tundra is disturbed or damaged there are fewer prey to hunt. Dangerous predators, such as polar bears, brown bears, and wolves, may go into towns to find food.

TUNDRA FUTURES

Tundra is a remarkable and fascinating biome. That's why people are taking action to protect tundra now and into the future.

Reserves

One way people protect tundra biomes is by creating reserves. In reserves, there are controls to limit building and mining. This ensures animals can migrate without having to cross roads and can raise young safely without being disturbed. Pollution can be prevented by banning industries, such as oil drilling.

When tourists visit reserves, their money is used to help the reserve and to pay the wages of local people. Visitors also learn about the biome and how to protect it. By only using marked paths and roads, for example, tourists reduce the damage to delicate tundra plants and soil.

Walkers rest near the mosses of alpine tundra in Svalbard, Norway. All plants are protected in this fragile natural setting, so tourists must take special care not to damage them.

Fact Focus: The Loss of Lichen

Lichens can be damaged and die if there is too much air pollution. When industries reduce air pollution, there are more tundra lichens for plant eaters, from tiny insects to caribou.

Changing energy use

Global warming is affecting all biomes and settlements on our planet in different ways. The biggest change that people can make to slow the warming is by reducing their use of fossil fuels. They can reduce power use, such as turning off lights when leaving rooms or using energy-efficient washing machines. People can use vehicles less by walking and cycling more, carpooling, and taking fewer flights. What can you do to help?

The Arctic National Wildlife Refuge is the biggest wildlife reserve in the USA and home to a huge variety of animals, including beautiful grizzly bears like these.

Fact File: Arctic National Wildlife Refuge

Location: Alaska, USA
Size: 30,125 square miles (78,050 km²)
Overview: A protected home to 250 species of animal, such as caribou, wolves, and polar bears. Oil companies want to drill in the coastal region because there is much oil beneath the ground.

GLOSSARY

adaptation Special feature or behavior that helps a living thing survive in its habitat

algae Living things similar to a plant that make their own food by photosynthesis

antifreeze Chemical added to water to stop it from freezing

Arctic Region including the North Pole, Arctic Ocean, and the land surrounding it

bacteria Tiny living things that can cause diseases or decompose waste

biome Region of Earth with living things adapted to the typical climate, soils, and other features

boggy Made up of wet, spongy ground

breed Have young

bud Plant part that contains young flowers, leaves, or shoots

camouflage Color, pattern, or shape that makes it hard to identify an object against its background

caribou Large, hairy animal with hooves and antlers, also known as reindeer

climate Typical weather pattern through the year in an area

decomposers Living things, such as bacteria and fungi, that break down waste and bits of dead plants and animals into nutrients

dissolve Mix a solid such as sugar or salt with a liquid such as water to create a solution

food chain A way of showing the movement of the sun's energy from one living thing to another

food web A network of related food chains that show how energy is passed from one living thing to another

fossil fuel Oil, gas, and coal, fuels which formed millions of years ago inside rocks from the remains of living things

fungi Type of living thing, such as mushrooms or yeasts

global warming Rise in average temperature of Earth caused by human activity, which is altering weather patterns

habitat Place where an animal or plant typically lives

hibernation Special type of deep sleep when body processes slow

Indigenous Peoples who have lived in a place for a very long time and have strong historical and cultural associations with it

insulation Layer that prevents the loss of heat from an object or living thing

lichen Life-form that is a partnership between two types of living things, fungi and algae

meltwater Water created when ice melts

migrate Move from one area to another due to seasonal changes

national park An area in nature where the wildlife is protected by law

natural resources Things found in nature that are useful to people, such as plants and water

nutrient Chemical substances essential for living things to be healthy, grow, and live

permafrost Deep layer of permanently frozen soil

pesticide Chemical used to kill pest insects and other animals

photosynthesis Process by which green plants make sugary food using the energy in sunlight

pollinate Transfer grains called pollen from one flower to another so a plant can make seeds

pollution Something that damages water, air or land or makes it harmful to living things

predator Animal that hunts and eats others

prey Animals hunted and eaten by others

reserve Area protected to keep living things and landscapes of interest safe from the harmful activities of people

scavenger Animal that feeds on dead things or waste

sedges Grass-like plants with tough stems

snowmobile Motorized sled

stilt Pole used to raise something above ground

surface area Area on the outside of an object

thaw Become liquid or soft after warming up

tissues A group of cells that form the structural materials of a plant or animal

treeline As you move northward, the line beyond which it is too dry or cold for trees to grow

FIND OUT MORE

Books
Arctic Research Journal (Ecosystems Research Journal)
Ellen Rodger
Crabtree Publishing, 2017

Tundras Inside Out (Ecosystems Inside Out)
James Bow
Crabtree Publishing, 2015

Baby Mammoth Mummy: Frozen in Time: A Prehistoric Animal's Journey into the 21st Century
Christopher Sloan
National Geographic Children's books, 2011

WEBSITES AND WEBCAMS

For more facts and information about tundra, go to:

www.ucmp.berkeley.edu/glossary/gloss5/biome/tundra.html

Arctic foxes are fascinating tundra animals. Learn more at:

www.arkive.org/arctic-fox/vulpes-lagopus/image-G58212.html

The caribou migration is remarkable. Find out more about it at:

www.fws.gov/refuge/arctic/carcon.html

Discover more about the traditional lives of Nenets people at:

http://bit.ly/2fnZPLT

Webcams
Watch polar bears going about their daily lives in the Arctic tundra, filmed from a buggy that carries scientists and tourists.

http://bit.ly/2nz1KVZ

Use a steerable webcam to look around an area of mountain tundra in Colorado.

instaar.colorado.edu/tundracam/

INDEX